HAPPY TIMES IN NOISY VILLAGE

Also by Astrid Lindgren

Noisy Village series
The Children of Noisy Village
Happy Times in Noisy Village
Christmas in Noisy Village (picture book)
Springtime in Noisy Village (picture book)

The Pippi Longstocking series
Pippi Longstocking
Pippi Goes on Board
Pippi in the South Seas

The Bill Bergson series
Bill Bergson, Master Detective
Bill Bergson Lives Dangerously
Bill Bergson and the White Rose Rescue

Karlsson series
Karlsson-on-the-Roof
Karlsson Flies Again

Emil series
Emil in the Soup Tureen
Emil's Pranks
Emil and the Piggy Beast

Others
Mischievous Meg
Ramus and the Vagabond
Seacrow Island

Picture Books
The Tompten (adapted)
The Tompten and the Fox (adapted)
Christmas in the Stable (with Harald Wiberg)
I Want to Go to School
I Want a Brother or Sister
The Runaway Sleigh Ride

And many others

HAPPY TIMES

IN NOISY VILLAGE

By Astrid Lindgren

Illustrated by Ilon Wikland

Translated by Florence Lamborn

Bethlehem Books • Ignatius Press
Bathgate, North Dakota   San Francisco

Bullerby Boken © 1961, by Astrid Lindgren.

Happy Times in Noisy Village © 1963 by The Viking Press.

Copyright renewed © Viking Penguin, a division of Penguin Books, USA, Inc., 1991.

This edition published in 2003 by Bethlehem Books by arrangement with Viking Children's Books, a division of Penguin Putnam Inc.

Cover art by Ilon Wikland
Cover design by Davin Carlson

First printing, June 2003

ISBN 1-883937-66-3
Library of Congress Card Number: 2003107127

Bethlehem Books • Ignatius Press
10194 Garfield Street South
Bathgate, North Dakota 58216
800 757 6831
www.bethlehembooks.com
Printed in the United States on acid-free paper

Contents

1. Noisy Village

MY NAME is Lisa, and I am a girl, as I have already told you. I have two brothers, who are both older than I am. Karl is eleven years old and Bill is ten. Soon I'll be ten myself, but so far I'm only nine.

We live on a farm called Middle Farm, because it is between two others. The other two are called North Farm and South Farm. Anna and Britta live at North

Farm, and they are girls too. Britta is eleven and — what luck— Anna is just my age.

A boy named Olaf lives at South Farm. Between his farm and ours is a large linden tree whose branches touch both houses at the upstairs windows. When the boys want to visit each other, they just climb through the tree.

Because there are so many children around making noise all the time, everyone calls the three farms Noisy Village. They are in a row like this:

My picture doesn't show our barn or the lake or the school, so you'll just have to imagine what they look like.

Sometimes we three girls play by ourselves without the boys, and sometimes the boys play without us. But usually we all play together, because most games are more fun when there are six instead of only three.

Olaf has a little sister named Kerstin who is still too

2

little to play with us. She is only a year and a half old, and I can remember when she was born. That's the first thing I want to tell you about.

2. Olaf Gets a Baby Sister

SOMETIMES when I get tired of Karl and Bill I think that it would be better not to have any brothers at all. They tease me when I play with my dolls; they're always boxing and hitting me; and they always say that it's my turn to dry the dishes. One time Karl said to Mommy that he couldn't understand why anyone should have wanted to have a girl. It would have been much better to have had nine more boys, so they could have enough for a soccer team. But Mommy said, "I am so happy to have my little girl. I don't know what I'd do without her. But nine more boys, heaven forbid! It's quite enough with you two."

So Karl didn't get anywhere with his stupid suggestion.

But sometimes it's nice to have brothers — when we have pillow fights at night, when they come into my room and tell ghost stories, and when it's Christmas and things like that. And once Bill stood up for me when a boy in school hit me because I pushed him by mistake. Bill hit him back and said, "Don't ever do that again!"

"Well, she doesn't have to push me," said Ben. That was the other boy's name.

"That wasn't her fault. She didn't see you. She doesn't have eyes in the back of her head, you dope," said Bill.

My, how I liked Bill then! So it really isn't too bad to have brothers, but, of course, it would be better to have sisters.

"The main thing is not to be an only child," Olaf used to say. Before Kerstin was born, he would get furious because he didn't have any brothers and sisters.

"Other people can have children, but in this house we never have any," he said angrily.

But then, over a year ago, a little sister came after all. Olaf was so happy. The day she was born he rushed in and said we had to come and look at her right away. So we did.

"There she is. Isn't she pretty?" Olaf said and looked terribly proud.

But she certainly *wasn't* pretty! She was all red and wrinkled and really looked awful, I thought. Never have I seen anyone so amazed as Karl was when he saw how

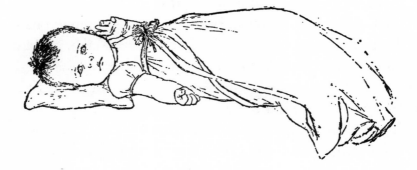

Olaf's baby sister looked. He stood there with his eyes popping and his mouth wide open. But he didn't say anything.

"Yes, she's very pretty," said Britta, and then we left.

Then Karl said, "Poor Olaf! Imagine having a sister like that! You can't say that Lisa is any beauty, but at least she looks like a human being. Imagine how embarrassed Olaf will be when this poor thing starts to school."

About a week passed before we went back to South Farm. Every day Olaf told us how pretty his little sister was, and Karl always looked so funny when he said it. But then we were all invited to South Farm for the christening.

"Oh, that poor child," said Karl on the way over. "It would probably be best for her if she could just die while she is a baby."

The dining room at South Farm looked lovely. There were flowers everywhere, because Olaf's sister had been born in the spring when there were primroses and lilies of the valley. There was a jug of birch leaves in the open fireplace, and the table was set. And Olaf was all dressed up. So were we. The minister stood in the dining room and waited. All of a sudden the door opened, and Aunt Lisa came in carrying Olaf's little sister. Oh, how that baby had changed! She had large, dark blue eyes, and her face was all pink, and her mouth — well, I just can't tell you what a pretty little mouth she had! She wore a beautiful long white christening dress.

Karl looked just as amazed as when he had seen her the first time. "Have you got a new one?" he whispered to Olaf.

"A new one? What do you mean?" said Olaf.

"A new baby," Karl said.

"What are you talking about?" said Olaf.

Then Karl didn't say anything more.

The minister christened Olaf's sister and named her Kerstin.

My, how I like Kerstin! She was the prettiest baby in the world. Anna and Britta and I used to run over to South Farm almost every day to watch while Aunt Lisa took care of her. How she wiggled and kicked! — not

Aunt Lisa, of course, but Kerstin. She looked so sweet.
She wiggled most of all when she had her bath. She

loved to take a bath. Sometimes, when she lay in her bassinet, she almost talked, and it sounded like "ba, ba." Olaf thought she would soon be able to say anything she wanted to. When Olaf went to the bassinet to look at Kerstin, she would smile just as if she were happy to see him. She didn't have any teeth, but she still looked sweet when she smiled. Olaf's eyes sparkled when he looked at her. Skipp was a little jealous of Kerstin. He wants Olaf to like him, of course. But Olaf petted Skipp a lot and told him he was a very good and fine dog, so Skipp wasn't jealous any more.

Once Aunt Lisa let Anna and me take care of Kerstin. Olaf wasn't home, thank goodness; otherwise, he would have wanted to take care of her himself. This is how it happened. Kerstin was lying in the bassinet, and started to cry like anything just as Aunt Lisa was about to take some loaves out of the oven. She was wet and hungry and mad — Kerstin, of course, not Aunt Lisa. So Aunt Lisa said, "Do you girls think you could bathe her?"

"Of course we could," we said.

Anna brought out the bathtub and poured water into it. Aunt Lisa came and tested the water with her elbow, and I lifted Kerstin out of her bassinet. And, do you know, she stopped crying at once and started laughing instead. When I held her close to me, she nibbled my cheek. It didn't hurt, because she didn't have any teeth, you know. My face got all wet, but that didn't matter.

Aunt Lisa has taught me how to hold babies. You should hold them so that their backs get support; I also know how you should hold them when you give them a bath, so they won't get their heads under the water. So I held Kerstin while Anna washed her with the washcloth. Kerstin wiggled and kicked and said, "Ba, ba." Then she tried to suck the washcloth, but we didn't let her!

"She's so cute that I could eat her up," said Anna.

Anna had put a blanket on the kitchen table, and a bath towel to dry Kerstin with. When I had finished bathing Kerstin, I put her on the blanket very carefully. We wrapped her in the towel, and Anna and I helped each other dry her. Then we sprinkled her all over with talcum powder. Suddenly Kerstin put her big toe in her mouth and started sucking it, but we had to take her toe away from her when we started to put on her little shirt. Aunt Lisa helped us to put on her diaper, because that was a little harder, but we put her pants on her by ourselves. When she was all ready, Aunt Lisa fed her.

Afterward Aunt Lisa let Anna and me take Kerstin for a ride in her carriage. We pretended that Anna was the daddy and I, the mommy, and Kerstin, our little baby. It wasn't long before Kerstin went to sleep. But we still pushed her around and had such fun. When Olaf came home, he rushed up and took away the carriage, just as if he had thought we were stealing Kerstin. But when he had pushed her carriage for a while, he let us hold the handle too and help push. We told Olaf that Kerstin had sucked her big toe, and Olaf laughed and said, "No one would believe how many tricks that child can do. Perhaps she'll be in the circus when she grows up."

Just then Kerstin woke up and looked at Olaf. He tickled her under the chin and said, "Well, well, you little rascal. So you were sucking your big toe, were you?" Then he laughed again and looked still more proud — just as if the finest thing you could do in this world was to suck your big toe.

3. Boys Just Can't Keep A Secret

EVERY year when it is time to harvest the hay, Daddy says, "This year I don't want any children up in the loft to trample the hay to pieces." But even though he always says this, nobody really believes that he means it.

So all day during the harvest we ride in the hay wagons and jump on the hay in the loft. This year Karl wanted to have a contest to see who dared jump the highest — jump the highest from the top down and not from the bottom up, of course. We climbed up on the beams under the roof and jumped down unto the hay underneath. My, how it tickled my tummy! Karl had said that the one who won the contest would get a lollipop as a prize. He had bought it that same day at the store in Big Village. We jumped and climbed and climbed and jumped, but finally Karl climbed up as high as he could and leaped down into a tiny little tuft of hay. He landed with a thud and lay still a long time without moving. Later he said he thought his heart must have fallen down into his tummy and that he would have it in his tummy as long as he lived. Nobody else dared jump from that high, so Karl stuck the prize in his mouth and said, "This lollipop to Karl for brave deeds in the hayloft!"

One day, after Britta and Anna and I had taken a ride in the haywagon with Kalle, the hired man from North Farm, we found a wild strawberry patch behind a pile of stones in a field where we were getting hay. I have never seen so many strawberries! We decided that we should never, never, never tell the boys, or anyone else, about

13

14

that strawberry patch. We picked strawberries and strung them on straws, until we had thirteen straws full. In the evening we ate them with sugar and cream. We gave Karl and Bill and Olaf each a couple, but when they wanted to know where we had picked them we said, "We'll never in the world tell you that, because it's a secret."

Then for several days Britta and Anna and I ran around looking for new strawberry patches and didn't bother to play in the hayloft. But the boys played there. We couldn't understand why they never got tired of it.

One day we said to the boys that now we had seven strawberry patches that we were never going to show them because it was a secret. Then Olaf said, "Haha, that certainly isn't much of a secret compared to ours!"

"What kind of a secret do you have?" said Britta.

"Don't tell her, Karl," Olaf said.

But Karl said, "Yes, I will. Then the girls can hear that our secret isn't as silly as theirs."

"What is it then?" we said.

"We have made nine caves in the hay, if you want to know," Karl said.

"But we won't tell you where," said Bill, and he hopped up and down on one leg.

"We'll soon find them," we said and rushed up into

the hayloft to look. We looked all that day and the next, but we didn't find any caves.

The boys thought they were so smart, and Karl said, "You'll never find them. In the first place, you can't find them without a map; and in the second place, you can't find the map."

"What kind of map is it?" we asked.

"A map that we have made," said Karl. "But we have hidden it." Then Britta and Anna and I started to look for the map instead of for the caves. We thought it must be hidden someplace at Middle Farm, because Karl surely would not have let them hide it anywhere else. We looked around in Karl's and Bill's room for hours. We looked in their beds, in their drawers, in their closet, and everywhere.

Finally we said to Karl, "You could at least tell us if it's bird, beast, or fish, the way you do when we play twenty questions."

And then Karl and Bill and Olaf started to laugh, and Karl said, "You may as well give up, because you'll never find the map anyway."

So we didn't look any more. But the next day I was going to ask Olaf if I could borrow *The Arabian Nights* from him, because it was raining and I wanted to stay indoors to read. Karl and Bill were outside, and I went into their room. I was going to climb through the linden tree into Olaf's window.

A little bird had lived in the tree before, and there was a hole in the trunk where he had had his nest. He didn't live there any longer, but when I climbed past his nest I saw a string hanging down from it.

What in the world did the bird use that string for? I thought, and pulled the string out. A roll of paper was tied to the end of the string. It was the map! I was so surprised, I thought I'd fall down out of the tree. I forgot all about *The Arabian Nights* and climbed back into Karl's and Bill's room. I ran over to Britta's and Anna's as fast as I could. I was in such a hurry that I tripped and fell on the stairs and hurt my knee.

My, how happy Britta and Anna were! We hurried to the hayloft with the map, and, before long, we found all the caves. Through the hay the boys had dug long tunnels which were all drawn on the map.

When you creep through one of those tunnels, and it's dark, and there is hay all around, you can't help thinking sometimes: what if I can't get out again? It feels scary and is awfully exciting. But you do always get out.

It was only in the tunnels that it was dark. In the caves it was light, because they were all next to the wall, and light came in through the cracks. They were big,

fine caves, and we realized that the boys must have had an awful job making them. The tunnel to the last cave was so long we thought it would never end. I crept through first, then Britta, and then Anna.

"I bet we've come into a labyrinth that will never end," said Britta.

But just then I saw that it started to get light in front of me, and there was the cave. And — ooh — there sat Karl and Bill and Olaf. You should have seen how surprised they looked when I stuck my nose through the entrance to the cave.

"How did you find your way here?" said Karl.

"Haha, we found the map, of course," I said. "That wasn't very hard."

For a minute Karl was a little put out. But when he had thought a while, he said, "O.K., let's let the girls play too!"

We played all day in the caves, while it rained outside, and had such fun. But the next day Karl said, "Now that you know our secret, you tell us your secret about your strawberry patches. It's only fair."

"That's what you think," we said. "You'll have to find

them by yourselves, just as we found your caves."

But to make it a little easier, Britta and Anna and I put arrows made of sticks on the ground. We put the arrows very far apart, though, so it still took the boys a long time to find the strawberry patches. We didn't put down any arrows to show the way to our very best patch. That's our secret, and we are never, never, never going to tell it to anyone.

4. We Start School Again

WHEN we've had summer vacation for a long time, I, at least, think it's very nice when school starts again. Bill says he is going to write to the king and ask him to close all the schools. I hope the king won't do that, because I like school. I like our teacher, and I like my friends. I like my schoolbooks too, when I've put nice new paper around them and pasted on labels with my name on them.

Karl and Bill don't like their books as much as I do, and they don't put new paper around them, unless Mommy or Miss Johnson tells them they have to. Also they draw pictures in their books. Karl cuts out faces from the comics — Dick Tracy and Nancy and all kinds of people like that — and pastes them on top of the pictures in his geography book. He says there is more variety that way. This I can really believe, because if it says under a picture "Chinese peasant planting rice," he is only

Chinese below the neck. His face is Dick Tracy's.

All of us children from the three farms walk to school together, and we have to leave home at seven o'clock in the morning, because it is so far. We carry sandwiches and milk to eat at school during lunch hour. But sometimes the boys eat up all their lunch on the way, before we ever get to school.

"You might just as well have your lunch in your stomach as in your schoolbag," Karl says.

Miss Johnson lives on the top floor of the schoolhouse. She has a nice room there with a piano, lots of books, and a cute little kitchen. We help her carry in wood for the stove. Sometimes she lets us borrow some books, and sometimes she treats us to chocolate.

Once when we got to school Miss Johnson was very sick, so we didn't have any school that day. All the other children knew about it, because they have telephones in Big Village, but in Noisy Village we don't have them, and we didn't know what to think when the schoolroom was locked and there were no children and no teacher. Finally, we went upstairs and knocked on Miss Johnson's door.

"Come in," Miss Johnson said.

We went in. There she lay in bed, and she was very sick. A lady was supposed to come to help her, but she

hadn't come. Then Miss Johnson asked if we would help her instead. Of course we said we would. The boys ran out to get wood, and Britta made a fire in the stove and put on some water to make tea. I swept the floor and shook Miss Johnson's pillows, and Anna set a tray. Then we treated Miss Johnson to tea and sandwiches.

Miss Johnson said she longed so terribly for some beef stew, and she had some meat. She wondered if we would be able to make it if she told us what we should do.

"We can always try," said Britta. "If it doesn't turn out to be beef stew, it'll probably be something else."

But it did turn out to be beef stew after all. Now I know how to make beef stew, and that's one thing I won't have to learn when I grow up. Miss Johnson asked us to try some, and it tasted very good. Afterward Britta washed the dishes; Anna and I dried them. Karl and Bill and Olaf sat on the floor by Miss Johnson's bookshelf the whole time and read books. Boys never are any good around the house. We stayed with Miss Johnson until the time school would have been out. When we started to leave, we asked her if she was going to be sick the next day too; she said she was. Then we wondered if she would let us come back and help her again. Miss Johnson said she would be very happy if we would come.

When Britta, Anna and I got there the next day, Miss

Johnson's bed was all rumpled, and, poor thing, she wanted some oatmeal. All of us together helped her to the rocking chair; then we made her bed nice and smooth, and when she had got back in it, she said that she felt like a princess. Then we made her some oatmeal, and afterward we gave her coffee and fresh coffee cake that I had brought from home. And then she said it was fun to be sick. Unfortunately, she was well the next day. Otherwise, we would have learned to cook still more dishes.

In the fall and winter it's dark when we go to school in the morning, and dark when we come home in the afternoon. It would be quite scary to walk that way all alone in the dark, but since there are six of us, it's just fun. We walk through the forest nearly the whole way, and Karl tries to make us believe that the forest is full of goblins and giants and witches. Perhaps it is, but we haven't seen any yet. Sometimes there are stars in the sky when we walk home. Karl says that there are two million five hundred thousand and fifty-four stars in the sky and that he knows the name of every one of them. I think he made that up, because once I asked him the name of a star, and he said it was "Large-finestar." But the next day when we walked home from school, I asked him about the same star, and then he said that it was called "The Queen's Crown."

"Yes, but yesterday you said that it was called Large-finestar," I said.

Then he said, "No, that wasn't this one. The Large-finestar fell down from the sky last night. The Queen's Crown is a different one. You can believe me!"

Sometimes when we walk home from school we sing— songs like "I walk through forests, mountains, and valleys." If someone should hear us, he would wonder who was singing, because it's so dark he couldn't see that it was only us children from Noisy Village.

5. Olaf Has A Loose Tooth

ONE DAY at school Miss Johnson said to Olaf, "Why do you keep putting your fingers in your mouth?"

He looked very embarrassed, and then he said, "I have a loose tooth."

"Pull it out, then, when you get home," said Miss Johnson. "But not now. We have to do arithmetic now. Tomorrow we will all look at the gap where the tooth was."

Olaf looked terrified, because he thinks it's scary to pull a tooth no matter how loose it is. I do too.

"My goodness, it won't hurt to pull out a little baby tooth like that," Daddy says.

Maybe it doesn't hurt so much, but it's still scary. Daddy gives us ten öre for every tooth he pulls out. Of course, he only pulls out the ones that are loose, but that's quite enough, because I think you almost always have a loose tooth. Bill isn't a bit afraid of pulling out his teeth, so he really shouldn't get ten öre when he pulls one. He just puts a heavy thread around the tooth, gives it a jerk, and the tooth is out. Daddy gives Bill ten öre anyway, because he is so brave.

But Olaf, poor thing, is more scared than I am of pulling teeth. He let us all feel his loose tooth when we were walking home from school. It was *really* loose.

"I can jerk that out for you in no time," Bill said.

"You're not jerking out anything," said Olaf. He hung his head all the way home and hardly said a word.

"Don't feel sad because you have a loose tooth," I said. "It's really nothing." I said this because it was Olaf's tooth and not mine. It's only when you have a loose tooth yourself that it's scary.

"I know," said Karl. "When we get home you can tie a piece of strong thread around the tooth, and we'll tie the other end to the fence. I'll heat an iron skewer until it's red hot and swish it back and forth right in front of your nose. Then you'll be so scared that you'll jump backward, and the tooth will pop out."

"Iron skewers indeed!" Olaf said angrily. He didn't like that idea at all. But he did tie a piece of strong black thread around his tooth when we got home, so he could pull at it from time to time and make the tooth still looser.

In some way he *had* to try to get rid of it, because Miss Johnson had said she was going to look at the gap the next day. I think that's what worried Olaf the most. He had to have the tooth out by the next day, or Miss Johnson would know that he was afraid of pulling teeth.

Anna tried to console him. She said, "Don't worry. Miss Johnson will probably forget all about your tooth by tomorrow."

But Anna knew just as well as Olaf that Miss Johnson never forgets anything. Karl says she has a memory like an elephant's.

We played ball down on the road, as we usually do on spring evenings, and the whole time the long black thread hung out of Olaf's mouth. It looked so funny when he ran. At times he forgot the tooth, and the thread, and the whole bother; then he laughed and talked as usual. But all of a sudden he would look sad and peculiar and would tug at the thread and sigh.

"It's crazy! It's only fastened by a thin little piece of skin. For goodness' sake, pull it out!" one of us would say.

Olaf shuddered when he heard this. It's that last little piece of skin that's the worst.

When we got tired of playing ball, we went up to Grandfather's and told him that Olaf had a loose tooth.

"He has to pull it out tonight," said Karl. "Because Miss Johnson wants to see the gap tomorrow."

Olaf almost started to cry when Karl said that.

"My, oh my," said Grandfather. "Speaking of teeth, I remember when I was a little boy—"

"Yes, Grandfather, tell about what happened when you were a little boy," Anna said and climbed up in his lap.

Then Grandfather said that when he was a little boy he had a terrible toothache for a whole month, until finally he went to the blacksmith to have the tooth pulled. There were no dentists where he lived. The blacksmith took a big pair of pliers and pulled out Grandfather's tooth, and it hurt terribly. But after Grandfather went home he got an awful toothache again, because the blacksmith had pulled the wrong tooth. Grandfather then had a toothache for another month, but he didn't dare go back to the blacksmith, because it hurt so to have big molars pulled with a pair of pliers. But, finally, the tooth ached so badly that he *had* to go back. That time the blacksmith pulled the right tooth, but he almost lifted Grandfather out of the chair to do it because the tooth had such big roots and was so hard to get out.

"Poor Grandfather," said Olaf.

I think that Olaf thought his own tooth was just as terrible to get out, although it didn't have any roots at all.

"Just imagine, Grandfather! You were once a little child afraid of having teeth pulled," Anna said.

"My, oh my, that was a long time ago," said Grandfather. "Now I only have three teeth left, and they'll fall out by themselves any day."

"So now you never have to be afraid again," Anna said.

"No, my little friend. I never have to be afraid again," said Grandfather.

Then he went to the corner cupboard and took out some barley-sugar for us. He gave us each a piece and said, "You shouldn't eat barley-sugar. It'll give you a toothache. My, oh my!"

Then we said good night to Grandfather and left.

"Well, how about your tooth?" Karl said. "Is it going to sit there until you get as old as Grandfather?"

Olaf got mad, and I don't blame him.

"Is it in your way?" he said. "After all, it's my tooth, isn't it?"

31

"Yes, but when are you going to pull it out?" said Britta.

Olaf tugged a little at the thread and said, "Tomorrow morning, maybe."

Then he ran home, and Karl said, "I feel sorry for Olaf. I know what I'll do. When he has gone to sleep I'm going to climb into his room and pull his tooth for him."

"But do you really think you could do that?" we said.

"Of course," he said. "Karl Erikson, D.D.S., extracts teeth under complete anesthesia."

Then we said we wanted to come along and look. So we all ran up to Karl's and Bill's room and waited. We heard Olaf fussing around with something in his room at the other side of the linden tree.

Finally Karl called, "Aren't you going to go to bed soon, Olaf?"

"Go to bed yourself," Olaf said.

"Bill and I are already in bed," Karl replied. We giggled quietly, because they were only lying on top of their beds and still had their clothes on.

"Aren't you sleepy, Olaf?" called Bill after a while.

"Yes, but you're making so much noise that I can't sleep," said Olaf. So we thought he must have gone to bed by then.

"Turn out the light, Olaf," Karl said.

"Turn out your own light," Olaf answered, and Karl

did. We sat in the dark and waited. After a while Olaf turned out his light.

"I hope he soon goes to sleep, because otherwise I will," said Anna, and yawned.

Just then we heard something rustle in the linden tree. It was Olaf on his way over to our house. Britta and Anna and I sneaked quickly into the closet. Karl and Bill crept down in their beds and pulled the covers up to their chins.

"Bill," said Olaf, while he climbed through the window. "I'll probably be sick tomorrow, so I won't be able to go to school. In that case, you don't need to wait for me."

"Sick! Why should you be sick?" Karl said. "If you went to bed in decent time, you'd be as healthy as a fish."

"I have a stomach ache," said Olaf and crept back to his room.

I'm sure he had a stomach ache just because he was so nervous on account of his tooth.

We waited a long, long time, and finally we were so sleepy that we could hardly keep our eyes open.

"He must have gone to sleep by now," Karl said at last. And then he crept out into the linden tree. "Are you awake, Olaf?" he said, as quietly as he could.

"No, I'm fast asleep," said Olaf.

So we had to sit down and wait some more. Finally Karl said he was going over to see if Olaf had gone to sleep. If he hadn't, there was something wrong with him, and then Karl would go and get the doctor. So we all crept through the tree as quietly as we could. Karl had brought his flashlight, and he flashed it on Olaf's bed. There he lay, fast asleep, with the black thread trailing out of his mouth. Oh, I got so scared! What if it hurt a

34

lot, and Olaf started to cry! What would he say when he saw all of us standing there?

Karl took a firm grip on the thread and whispered, "One, two, three, pull!"

And just as he said "Pull" he pulled—and there hung the tooth, dangling on the thread. Olaf didn't even wake up. He just mumbled in his sleep, "I have a stomach ache."

Bill tried to wake him up, but he couldn't. Karl said it was just as well, because now Olaf would think a ghost had been in his room and pulled his tooth. Karl tied the string to the light fixture in the ceiling, and there the tooth hung where it would be the first thing Olaf would see when he woke up. How happy he would be!

Olaf didn't have a stomach ache the next day. He was standing outside his gate and waiting for us, as usual. He laughed, so you could see a gap in his upper jaw.

"Was it you who did it, Karl?" he asked.

And then we told him that we had all been in his room. Olaf laughed still more when he heard what he had said in his sleep. He was so happy that he jumped up and down and kicked all the stones that lay in the road. Then he said, "It really isn't too bad to have teeth pulled."

"No, not under anesthesia," said Karl.

We decided that we'd pull out one another's teeth at

night. Well, I mean the loose ones, of course.

When we got to school, Olaf went right up to Miss Johnson, opened his mouth wide, and said, "Look, Miss Johnson. I pulled out my tooth!"

"I'm the one who did, to be more truthful," Karl mumbled at his desk. But Miss Johnson didn't hear him.

6. The Chest of the Wizards

OLAF was as careful with the tooth that Karl had pulled out as if it had been a gold nugget. He kept it in a matchbox in his pocket, and from time to time he took it out and looked at it.

A couple of days later Bill had a loose tooth. It would have been the easiest thing in the world for him to pull it out himself. But Bill decided that he also wanted to have it pulled out while he was sleeping. So he tied a long piece of strong string to his tooth just before he went to bed, and then he tied the other end to the knob of his door. The next morning when Agda came to wake up the boys and opened the door, the tooth popped out. Bill woke up even without Agda's having to shake him.

"It's strange how much fun you can have with teeth," Bill said as we walked to school that day. He too had put his tooth in a matchbox, and he and Olaf were comparing teeth most of the way.

Karl was cross because he didn't have a tooth that had been pulled out. But he said, "I wonder where I put that molar that the dentist in Big Village pulled last year."

In the evening he looked through his drawers for the tooth and found many valuable things that he had thought were lost forever. In a cigar box he found some chestnuts, several cartridge cases, a broken whistle, five broken tin soldiers, a broken fountain pen, a broken watch, and a broken flashlight, and then his molar. It was broken too. That was why it had been pulled. Karl looked at all these broken things and said that he would mend them all sometime. Well, maybe not the tooth. He put it in a matchbox instead. All that evening Karl and Bill and Olaf went around rattling their matchboxes and acting so smart. They didn't even want to play ball. So Britta and Anna and I played hopscotch and didn't pay any attention to them.

"I'm so tired of hearing about teeth at this point that I'm ready to pull out my own," Britta said.

Just then the boys came out. They had been up in Karl's and Bill's room a long time, and they looked full of mischief.

"Don't ever tell the girls, whatever you do," Karl said.

"I should say not! That would be a fine thing if *they* were told," said Bill.

"We'll never tell them in a month of Sundays!" Olaf said.

We were so curious that we were ready to burst, but we didn't let on at all.

"Anna, it's your turn now," I said.

We played hopscotch for dear life and pretended that we didn't even want to know whatever it was they were talking about.

The boys sat down by the side of the road and watched us.

"I hope you hid it really well," Bill said to Karl.

"Don't worry," Karl said. "The Chest of the Wizards is something that you have to hide very carefully."

"Yes, because otherwise the girls might find it," Olaf said, "and that would be a calamity."

"Olaf, please don't say such dreadful things!" he said. "If the girls should find it—Ye gods!"

"Lisa, it's your turn now," Britta said.

We kept on playing hopscotch, pretending that we hadn't heard a word about the Chest of the Wizards.

Then the boys left. They walked down the road in a row, one behind the other. Anna pointed to them and whispered, "There go the Wizards, haha!" And we laughed and laughed.

Karl turned around and said, "It's good that you can

keep your spirits up even though there are so many things in this world you know nothing about, you poor little things."

Then we decided that we would look for the Chest of the Wizards. We understood that it was just one of the boys' silly tricks, but we still wanted to find out where it was.

The boys had gone over to the pasture to ride Blossom, our black mare. So we rushed up to Karl's and Bill's room to hunt for the Chest. My, how we hunted. But it's not so easy to find the Chest of the Wizards when you don't even know what it looks like. We looked in the drawers and under the beds and on the shelves and in the fireplace and all over the attic. But we didn't find the Chest of the Wizards anywhere.

When we were right in the middle of our search, we heard the door to the attic open and the boys come stamping up. Did we move fast! There are a lot of clothes hanging in the attic, so we hid behind them and stood very, very still—just as quiet as mice.

"Let's take it out and look at it again," said Bill.

"First let's see where the girls are," Karl answered. "They're probably in Lisa's room, playing some silly old doll game."

"No, if they were, we could hear them, couldn't we?"

Olaf said. "They're all probably over at North Farm. Come on, take out the Chest!"

We stood there and didn't dare move. I was afraid that I would have to sneeze or that I would start laughing. Then it looked as if Karl would walk right into me, and I thought, oh, now I'll die! But he stopped just in time and bent down and lifted up something; I couldn't see what. Anna poked me, and I poked her back.

"Wizards, do you swear never to give away the hiding place?" Karl said.

"We swear never to let the unfaithful get hold of the Chest of Wizards," Bill and Olaf answered.

Of course, Britta and Anna and I were the "unfaithful," so I poked Anna again.

"Yes, because if the unfaithful get hold of it, it will lose its secret powers," said Karl.

I wanted so much to see this remarkable Chest, but the boys were standing right in front of it. Finally Karl put it back where it had been under a loose board. Then they clumped down the stairs again.

Suddenly we came to life. As soon as the attic door was closed, we rushed out and pulled away the board. And there was the Chest of the Wizards! Well, what do you know—it was nothing but Karl's old cigar box! THE CHEST OF THE WIZARDS was written on the cover in large letters, and under that was drawn a skull and crossbones.

"Hurry and open it, Britta, so we can see what wonderful treasures are inside," Anna said.

Britta did, and Anna and I stuck out our necks as far as we could, and all we saw were three white teeth—two little ones and a bigger one. That was all there was in the Chest of the Wizards.

"Sometimes I wonder if boys are quite right in their heads," said Britta.

Then we saw Agda's bureau standing there in the attic. Mommy had said that we were not, under any circumstances, to touch the bureau. But Agda is so nice. Sometimes she opens the bureau and shows me all the fine things she has in it. She has a little pink pincushion with lace, many pretty postcards with flowers on them, a perfume bottle that smells good, a bracelet made of gold, almost, and—well, there is so much that I can't tell you everything.

Last year when the dentist was in Big Village, he made Agda a set of new false teeth. He said that he had never seen such ugly false teeth as her old ones. It was too bad to have such ugly teeth when you looked so nice other-wise, he said. But Agda didn't throw away the old teeth when she got the new ones. She said to me that perhaps she could use them on weekdays, or when the weather was bad, and save the new ones for Sundays.

"These teeth are certainly good enough to wear while I'm feeding pigs and milking cows," she said.

But she soon got tired of the old teeth, because the new ones were so much prettier. Also Agda likes Oscar, our hired man, so she wants to look nice on weekdays too.

I knew that Agda kept the old teeth in the top drawer of her bureau, and that gave me an idea.

"I'll tell you what we can do," I said to Britta and Anna. "Let's put Agda's false teeth in the Chest of the Wizards. If the Chest could get secret powers from three puny little baby teeth, just think what it could get from a whole set!"

Britta and Anna thought that was a wonderful idea. It was much better than stealing the Chest of the Wizards, Britta said.

So we put Agda's teeth in the cigar box and put it back under the board. Then we went to look for the boys. They were way down the road, shooting marbles. We sat down beside them in the road and watched them.

"Well, well, so the Wizards are shooting marbles this beautiful evening," said Britta.

They didn't answer. Karl had his hands full of marbles, and I said, "The Chest of the Wizards would be a good place to keep the marbles in, I'll bet."

They still didn't answer, but Karl gave a deep sigh. You could tell that he thought the unfaithful were even more stupid than usual.

"Can't you tell us about the Chest of the Wizards?" Anna asked and poked Karl in the ribs.

But Karl said it was nothing you could tell girls. The Chest of the Wizards was full of secret powers. Only the secret society that owned the chest was allowed to know where it was. "Otherwise, it would lose its powers," he said.

"The secret society—is that you and Bill and Olaf?" Britta asked.

Karl kept quiet and looked mysterious. But Britta and Anna and I started to laugh with all our might.

"I think they're peeved because they don't know where we keep the cigar—uh—the Chest of the Wizards," Bill said.

"I bet it's in your closet," said Britta slyly.

"I bet it isn't," Bill said.

"Is that so? Then I bet you it's under a loose board in the attic floor," Anna said.

"I bet it isn't," said the boys all at the same time. But did they look worried! Their game of marbles got all confused.

"Let's go and look at your birds' eggs, Bill," said Karl.

Did he really think we believed that's what they'd do? We knew good and well they were going to run and get the Chest of the Wizards.

"My birds' eggs! Why, you've seen them a hundred times," said Bill. He is a little slow sometimes. Karl glared at him, and Bill finally understood.

"Oh, yes, of course, let's go and look at my birds' eggs," he said.

The boys left us then—slowly, so that we wouldn't suspect anything. We didn't leave slowly, though. We ran

over to Olaf's and told his mother that we were going to get something in his room. Then we rushed up the stairs and climbed through the linden tree to Karl's and Bill's room and ran into the attic and hid behind the clothes. We had just got there when the boys came clumping up the stairs.

"What do you think Anna meant about the attic floor?" Bill said. "Does she know anything?"

"No," said Karl. "That was just something to say. But we'd better move the Chest of the Wizards to another hiding place just to be on the safe side."

We couldn't see anything, because the boys were standing between us and the Chest, but we heard Olaf say, "Open it so I can look at my tooth."

"I want to look at mine too," said Bill.

"Wizards," Karl said, "what is hidden in this Chest must never be seen by the unfaithful. Only by us."

Then it got quiet, and we knew that Karl was lifting the lid. Then we heard a loud howl, so they must have caught sight of Agda's teeth. And we ran out from behind the clothes and laughed, and I said, "Now I bet you have enough powers to last you a whole year." Britta and Anna and I laughed again.

Karl threw Agda's teeth across the attic floor and said that girls should never have been born, because they always spoil everything.

Anna said, "Karl, please make a miracle for us with the cigar box!"

"Do you want a beating?" said Karl.

Then Karl and Bill and Olaf threw away their teeth, and we all went out and played ball.

7. *Karl Falls into the Lake*

IF YOU run right through the cow pasture at North Farm, you come to a little lake where we skate in the winter. Last year there was lovely glassy ice on the lake. One day Mommy didn't want us to go to the lake, because Daddy and Uncle Erik had cut out a large hole to get ice for all of us. But I said, "They put juniper branches around the hole, so we'll know where it is and keep away from it."

So she let us go.

Sometimes Karl is rather silly, especially when he tries to show off as he did that day on the ice. He skated as close to the hole as he could.

"Here comes the Master Skater from Noisy Village," he cried. He skated straight toward the hole and did not turn off until the very last moment.

"Stop it, Karl, you're really acting like a goof," said Olaf. We all bawled him out, but it didn't help.

"Here he comes, the brave Master Skater from Noisy Village," he said again.

Well, he certainly did come! In fact he splashed right down into the hole because he had come too close to the edge. We all screamed. And Karl screamed too, worse than anyone else. We got frightened and thought he would drown. Then we lay down on the ice in a long line and held on to each other's feet. Bill was at the head of the line, right at the edge of the hole, and with all of us holding him, he pulled Karl up out of the hole. Karl *almost* cried but not quite. We ran home as fast as we could.

"Just think if we had brought you home drownded," Bill said.

"You don't say 'drownded,' stupid," Karl answered. But I still think he liked Bill for pulling him out, because later in the afternoon he gave him a whole set of tin soldiers.

Mommy was quite angry at Karl for falling into the hole. He had to go to bed and drink hot milk. And afterward Mommy made him stay in bed several hours— to think about his sins, she said.

But that evening Karl got up to play with us in the snow. We built snow forts out in the yard and had a snowball battle. The girls had one fort, and the boys had another. But the boys made such hard snowballs and threw them so fast, that I didn't think it was fair. They came storming toward our fort with their hands full of snowballs, and Karl cried, "Battle and victory! Here comes the Terror of the Northland!"

So Britta said, "So that's who it is! Here I thought it was the Master Skater from Noisy Village!"

After that Karl didn't say anything for quite a while.

The boys captured our fort and made us prisoners and said we had to sit and make snowballs for them all evening.

"What are you going to do with all those snowballs?" Anna said.

"Save them until Midsummer, because then they are very rare," Karl said.

"Oh, go jump in the lake again," Anna said.

And then Britta and Anna and I got cold, so we went down to the barn. It was nice and warm in there. We played catch, and before long the boys came down too. The cows stared at us all the time. I don't think that cows can understand why you play catch. Come to think about it, I don't understand it either, but it sure is fun.

After a little while, Daddy came to the barn. He said we couldn't play catch any longer, because one of the cows was about to have a calf, and there mustn't be any noise and confusion. We stayed until it was born. It was a little bull calf, and he was so sweet. Lotta licked him and looked very happy. Daddy wanted us to help him think of a name for the calf.

"Let's call him the Terror of the Northland," Karl said.

What a stupid name for such a dear little calf! I don't think Karl can think of anything else except old Terror of the Northland.

"Well, he'll be a fierce, dangerous bull when he grows up, won't he?" Karl said.

Then Olaf suggested that we call the calf Peter, and Daddy thought that that would be a good name.

"Let's at least call him Peter from the Northland," Karl said.

Then we ran over to tell Grandfather that Lotta had a calf.

Very soon after that it was bedtime. Karl and Bill and I were standing in the attic, and I was about to go into my room, when Karl teased Bill and said, "I guess I'm lucky not to be 'drownded,' after all."

"Oh, go jump in the lake," said Bill.

8. We Go To School and Fool Miss Johnson

ON THE first of April we had fun fooling Miss Johnson, as you should on April Fool's Day. Well, perhaps you *shouldn't* do it, exactly, but you *can* do it, and you don't get punished for doing it.

Usually we start school at eight o'clock in the morning, but the day before April the first we all decided to go to school at six the next morning. Just before Miss Johnson locked the door of the schoolroom after our last lesson, Karl ran in and moved the hands of the clock in the schoolroom two hours ahead.

The next day we all got to school at six o'clock, but the clock on the wall in the schoolroom said eight.

We made all the noise we could outside the schoolroom door so that Miss Johnson would hear us. When she didn't come, Karl ran up to the second floor and knocked on her door.

"Who is it?" asked Miss Johnson, in a sleepy voice.

"It's Karl," he said. "Aren't we going to have any school today?"

"My goodness, I've overslept," said Miss Johnson. "I'll be down in a minute."

Miss Johnson has a clock up in her room too, of course, but she was in such a hurry that she forgot to look at it.

The clock in the schoolroom said twenty minutes past eight when Miss Johnson came down to let us in.

"I can't understand why my alarm clock didn't ring and wake me up," she said.

My, how hard it was for us to keep from laughing! We had arithmetic for the first lesson. And just as we were reciting the multiplication table, we heard the alarm clock ringing up in Miss Johnson's room. It was really seven o'clock then. But the clock in the schoolroom showed nine.

"What now?" said Miss Johnson.

"April fool! April fool!" we all yelled.

It's only on the first of April that you can say things like that to your teacher.

"Such children!" Miss Johnson said.

When we had had all the lessons that we were supposed to have that day, we thought, of course, that we would be allowed to go home, although it was only one o'clock. But then Miss Johnson said, "April fool! Now we'll have school for another hour."

So we had to stay for another hour. But it didn't matter, because Miss Johnson read stories to us.

On our way home Olaf suddenly said to Karl, "Why Karl, how did you get that big hole in the seat of your pants?"

Karl turned his head almost clear around trying to see the hole. When he had been looking for a while Olaf said, "April fool! April fool!"

Olaf was so pleased that he had been able to fool Karl. And he was still in the mood for fooling people when we met that mean shoemaker who lives halfway between Big Village and Noisy Village—the one whose name is Kind, but who isn't kind.

"Look, Mr. Kind," said Olaf. "Look at the fox over there in the bushes!"

But Mr. Kind didn't even look over that way; he only said, "And look at the bunch of trouble-making brats walking down the road."

Then Karl laughed.

In the afternoon, when we had done our homework, Karl ran over to South Farm and said to Olaf, "There's a scrap dealer over at North Farm and he's buying stones."

"He buys stones?" said Olaf, who had completely forgotten that it was April Fool's Day. "What kind of stones?"

"The kind of stones you have here in your garden I suppose," said Karl.

Olaf started picking up stones for dear life and putting them in a sack. Then he lugged the sack over to North Farm. There really was an old man over there, but he only bought empty bottles and other kinds of scrap.

"Here are some more stones for you," said Olaf. He pulled the sack up to the old man, looking pleased with himself.

"Stones?" said the old man. "Did you say stones?"

"Sure," said Olaf, and looked still more pleased. "First-class granite too. I've picked them myself in our garden."

"Is that so?" said the old man. "Well, then I can tell you that you have really struck stone, my little friend."

Then Olaf remembered that it was April Fool's Day. He got very red in the face and took his sack and dragged it home without saying a word. But Karl stood behind the fence and yelled, "April fool! April fool!" so loudly you could hear him all over Noisy Village.

9. *I Get A Baby Lamb*

ANNA and I sometimes try to figure out at which time of year we have the most fun. Anna thinks we have the most fun in the summer, and I think in the spring—except for Christmas, of course.

Now I'm going to tell you about one thing that happened last spring. We have a lot of sheep here in Noisy Village, and in the spring the ewes get baby lambs. The lambs are very cute—cuter than kittens or puppies or piglets.

During the time when the sheep have their babies, we run down to the sheep barn every morning to see how many new lambs have been born during the night. As soon as you open the door, all the sheep begin to baa very sweetly and not at all like the ewes and the ram, whose voices are loud and deep.

One Sunday morning when I went down to the sheep barn, I found a baby lamb dead in the straw. I ran and

told Daddy right away, and he found out why the lamb had died. His mother didn't have any milk to give him. I sat down on the threshold of the sheep barn and cried to think about the poor baby lamb. Anna came over, and when I told her about it, she cried too.

"I don't want baby lambs to die," I said to Daddy.

"Nobody does," Daddy said. "And I'm afraid there's still another one that won't live very long." And he showed us a little lamb that he was carrying in his arms. It was the dead lamb's brother and, of course, he couldn't get any milk from his mother either. When we heard this, Anna and I started crying even more.

"I don't want the little lamb to die," I cried and threw myself on the ground.

Daddy lifted me up and said, "Don't cry, Lisa." Then he said, "I'll tell you what, you may try to feed this lamb with a bottle, just as you would a baby."

I don't think I'd ever been so happy before! I didn't know that you could feed lambs the way you do babies. Daddy said not to be too sure. He thought that the lamb would probably die anyway, but we could always try.

Anna and I ran down to Aunt Lisa's and borrowed a nipple and a bottle that Olaf had drunk from when he was a baby. Then we ran back to Daddy again.

"Daddy, can't we give him a little cream, the poor thing," I said.

But Daddy said that his tummy could only take milk that was mixed with water. Then I stuck the nipple in the lamb's mouth, and he started to suck right away he was so hungry.

"Now you are the foster mother of this little lamb," said Daddy. "But he has to have food early and late, so you mustn't get tired of feeding him."

Anna said that if I did get tired she would do it for me. But I said, "Don't worry. No one could get tired of feeding a baby lamb."

I named the lamb Pontus, and Daddy said that he was my very own. It was lucky that all this was decided before Karl and Bill woke up that Sunday morning.

"To think that you can't even sleep late one morning without Lisa's getting a baby lamb!" said Karl, who was a little mad because he hadn't got Pontus.

The first few days every child in the Village went with me to feed Pontus, but, before long, they got tired of it.

It's strange how hungry baby lambs are. Every morning, before I went to school, I would run down to the sheep barn to give Pontus his bottle. As soon as he saw me coming, he would run toward me, wagging his short little tail and baaing so sweetly. He was all white, but he had a little black spot on his nose, so you could easily tell him from the other lambs. Agda fed him during the day when I was at school. I gave him another bottle as soon as I got home. And late at night he had to be fed again.

I had promised Daddy that I wouldn't get tired of feeding Pontus, and I didn't, because I loved him so much. I loved him mainly because he was so happy when he saw me. I think he thought that I was his real mother. I asked Karl and Bill if they thought this was so, and Karl said, "Yes, I'm sure he thinks so. You do look very much like a sheep."

One day Daddy said that it was time to try to teach Pontus to drink his milk from a bowl. He was getting too big to drink from a bottle.

Poor Pontus didn't know what he was supposed to do when I suddenly came and put a bowl under his nose. He nuzzled me to see where I had put the bottle.

Bill was watching.

"Drink the milk, for goodness sake," he said to Pontus. "Are you stupid or something?"

I got furious with Bill. "Pontus is certainly not stupid," I said. "You just don't understand baby lambs."

But Pontus just sniffed at the milk and baaed and looked sad. Then I found the trick! I dipped my hand in the milk, and when I put my fingers in Pontus' mouth he started to suck them. He sucked and he sucked, and, in that way, he drank all the milk—except for what he

spilled. So for a while Pontus drank by sucking my fingers.

But one morning, when he was very hungry and couldn't get the milk from my fingers fast enough, he started drinking from the bowl. After that he always drank from the bowl. In a way this was too bad, because he was so cute when he stood there and sucked the milk from my fingers.

A little later in the spring, the sheep were let out in the pasture to graze. The lambs were supposed to learn to eat grass, but they still had to have milk too, so I went to the sheep pasture every day with the bowl of milk. I would stand at the gate and yell "Pontus!" as loudly as I could. Then I would hear a little baaing way in the back

of the pasture, and Pontus would come running toward me at full speed, wagging his tail back and forth.

But Pontus has grown so big now that he doesn't drink milk any more; he just eats grass and munches leaves. He is such a good lamb and eats so well that he will surely grow up to be a big strong ram some day.

Perhaps one day I'll get another lamb or perhaps a dog or cat or a rabbit. But none of them will be as nice as Pontus. I'll never, never, never like any pet as well as I like Pontus!

10. Pontus Goes to School

KARL used to tease me and always say, "But it would be better to have a dog than a lamb."

Olaf agreed with him, of course, because he has a dog himself.

"Naturally it's better to have a dog," Olaf said.

"Why, may I ask?" I said.

"Well, for one thing, you can take a dog with you wherever you go," Olaf said.

"All Pontus does is run around in the sheep pasture," Karl said.

"But a lamb is much cuter," said Anna to help me out.

"A lot of good that does you," Karl said, "when he only runs around the pasture."

One morning after we had been talking about this the day before, I went, as usual, to the sheep pasture and called Pontus. When he came running he looked so cute that I thought I wouldn't trade him for a thousand dogs.

I also thought it was a shame that he ran around in the sheep pasture all the time with no one to see how cute he was. Then I thought about Skipp.

Sometimes he follows Olaf to school. That's why Olaf said that dogs go with you everywhere. And once Miss Johnson let Skipp come into the schoolroom and lie on the floor by Olaf's desk.

But with poor Pontus it was quite different; he had to stay in the sheep pasture all day. While he drank his milk, I thought about how unfair it was that dogs were allowed to go everywhere but not lambs. By the time Pontus had finished his milk, I had decided to let him come with me to school.

It's always hard for me to get ready in time for school when I have to go out and feed Pontus first. And on the morning when I was going to take him to school with me, I was so far behind that all the other children stood waiting for me outside Olaf's gate.

"Hurry up, Lisa," Britta called, "or we'll be late!"

Then I turned around and said to the lamb, "Hurry up, Pontus, or we'll be late!"

Never have I seen any children look as surprised as they did when they saw Pontus!

"Where—where is he going?" said Karl.

"To school," I said "And then perhaps we won't have

to hear any more that only dogs can go places."

"Lisa, are you quite sure that you're not feeling sick?" said Karl.

"Do Mommy and Daddy know about it?" Bill said.

When Bill asked that, I got a little worried, because it was something I hadn't thought about. But Anna clapped her hands and laughed and said, "Why shouldn't lambs be allowed to go along to school as well as dogs?"

And all of a sudden Karl started to smile, and he said,

"Let him come along; Miss Johnson will probably faint."

So then we trotted down the hills, all of us—Pontus too. Sometimes he stopped as if he wondered if this really was all right. But then I called "Pontus!" and he said "Baaa!" very sensibly and came along behind us.

It took us a little longer than usual to get to school, and we were late. The bell had already rung, and the other children had gone in.

Pontus stumbled going up the school steps, so I had to help him a little.

"Perhaps he isn't mature enough for school yet," Karl said.

When Karl first started to school several years ago, he couldn't sit still a minute. So Miss Johnson said that he wasn't mature enough for school yet and sent him home. She said that he could come back the next year, but first he had to play at home a little longer. Karl has never forgotten this. That's why he said that about Pontus.

Britta knocked on the school door, and we went in.

"I'm sorry we're late," said Britta.

As soon as she had said it, Olaf started to giggle as if someone were tickling him.

"My, but you seem happy today, Olaf," said Miss Johnson.

Pontus stood in the back where no one could see him, but of a sudden he said a little "Baa!" and stuck his head between my leg and Karl's. All the children jumped out of their seats. Miss Johnson did too, for that matter.

"What in the world—" she said. "You don't mean that you've brought a lamb to school?"

"Lisa—" Bill started, but then he was quiet, because he was afraid Miss Johnson would get mad at me. I was beginning to get a little scared myself.

"Because we're studying about domestic animals," I said, "I thought perhaps—"

"What did you think?" asked Miss Johnson.

"That it would be a good thing for the class to see a real lamb," I said. But I really hadn't thought about it until just that minute.

Miss Johnson started to laugh like everything, and all the children too, especially Olaf. He laughed until he almost choked.

Then we took Pontus up to Miss Johnson's desk, and all the children were allowed to come and pet him. We read about sheep in our nature study book, and I told

71

how I had raised Pontus with a bottle. Everyone liked him so much, and we sang "Baa, baa, black sheep" to him. I think Pontus himself was getting tired of all the noise and wanted to go back to the sheep pasture. But he was good and stayed very still beside my desk during the rest of the lesson. Well, sometimes he took a few small leaps and baaed. Every time he did, Olaf started to laugh so that all the other children had to laugh too.

When the weather is warm and sunny we always eat our sandwiches on the school steps during lunch hour. We did that day. As usual I had brought milk in a bottle, so I gave it to Pontus in a bowl I had borrowed from Miss Johnson. Anna gave me half of her milk so that I wouldn't be without any.

Afterwards Pontus ran around the schoolyard. Once he started nibbling a few of the carrots that were starting to sprout in Miss Johnson's vegetable garden, but I chased him away from there and told him that he'd have to calm down until he got home.

When school was over and we were going home, Karl said, "Tomorrow we are going to study about cattle. That'll be fun, and I'll bring the bull."

Then Olaf laughed until he got the hiccups.

"But it might be a little crowded to have him next to my desk," Karl said.

Miss Johnson had said that now we had brought enough live animals to school. It could be a help when you were studying about them, but it would be pretty confusing in the long run, she had said.

Pontus got tired on the way home, so we took turns carrying him up all the hills. Then we all went to take him to the sheep pasture. Never have I seen a lamb jump as high as Pontus did when we let him go! He galloped over to the other sheep and baaed so that you could hear him all over the pasture.

"It's quite clear that he isn't mature enough for school yet," Karl said.

11. Karl Captures Musk Oxen

THERE are two things I'm jealous of Britta and Anna about. The first is Grandfather. He says that with as few children as there are here in Noisy Village, he can easily be a grandfather to all of us. But then Anna says, "That may be, but you're still only my grandfather, really and truly. And Britta's too, of course!"

So when we're reading the paper to Grandfather, it's always Anna who gets to sit in his lap, and he calls her "my little friend." I can't understand how he can tell the difference between Anna and the rest of us when he's almost blind. But he can. Yet Anna isn't hairy like that Esau in the Bible. It was no trouble for Esau's daddy to tell his children apart when one of them was hairy and the other smooth. Grandfather is really clever, I think— especially since Anna isn't a bit hairy. Still, Grandfather is so very nice to all of us that it really doesn't make much difference that Anna is the one he calls "my little friend."

But Britta and Anna also have a lake of their own right next to their cow pasture. That's the other thing I'm jealous of. We go swimming there in the summer, and it has a lovely sandy beach.

On the other side of the lake there is no sandy beach, but there are high mountains. At least, I think they're high. We pretend that the mountains on the other side of the lake are the Rocky Mountains, and we row over there in the North Farm rowboat.

Karl says that a giant must have thrown all those big boulders and rocks around in our Rocky Mountains. That was a long time ago when there were no people, and no Noisy Village. I'm glad that I didn't live then, when there was no Noisy Village. Then we wouldn't have had any place to live. Karl says we would have had to live in the cave in the Rocky Mountains. There is one very big cave over there under a couple of huge boulders.

We always tie the rowboat to a certain pine when we get to the other side of the lake. Then we climb the mountains, but in our own special way. We have certain places where we can put our feet. This is necessary, because it is so hard to climb mountains. We have one crevice that we call the Nosescraper because it's so narrow that you almost always scrape your nose when you're going through it. But you *have* to go through the

Nosescraper. There is no other way. Then you go past a rock that juts away out, where you have to step on a very narrow ledge to get by. We call it the Armbreaker, because Karl says that once Bill fell down there and broke off his arm. Bill says that isn't so. Well, he did fall down, and he *nearly* broke his arm, but he certainly didn't break it off. But we call the rock the Armbreaker anyway. The most dangerous part we call the Dead Man's Hand. If you fall down there, you'd have to be wheeled home in a wheelbarrow, Karl says, because you'd be dead. When you've got past all those difficult places, you're almost up on top of the highest mountain. And then, if you walk a little way toward the forest, you come to the big cave we call the Rumble-hole.

One Sunday, just before school was out last spring, we took a trip to the Rocky Mountains. We took a picnic lunch and told our mothers that we would probably be gone all day.

Karl tied the rowboat to the pine we always use, and then we started to climb. We talked about which was the most fun, climbing mountains or climbing trees. And we all thought that it was just a little bit more fun climbing mountains.

After we had been through Nosescraper and Armbreaker and were climbing over Dead Man's Hand,

I shivered a little because it was so exciting. Karl looked down into the depths and said, "Everyone who intends to fall down here put up a hand or a foot!"

We certainly couldn't put up any hands or feet, because we needed them to hold on with, and, besides, nobody intended to fall down. Soon we were at the Rumble-hole.

We laid out our picnic lunch in a beautiful clearing in the woods right next to the Rumble-hole. You always get hungry right away when you're outdoors, so we all thought we might as well eat. We had pancakes—about a hundred—with us, and jam, milk, fruit juice, sandwiches, and cookies.

Then we went into the cave. Karl said that perhaps people had lived there during the Stone Age. My, but they must have been cold in the winter! There were large openings between the rocks, where the snow could blow in.

Britta suggested that we should pretend we were Stone-Age people. Karl thought that was a wonderful idea. He said that he and Bill and Olaf would go out to capture musk oxen, that Britta and Anna and I should stay in the cave and keep the food warm. Isn't that always the way? No matter what we play, the boys get to do something that's fun while we stay and keep the food warm and things like that. Britta said we could take bunches of leaves to sweep the cave with, and then we could put some pretty birch branches in the cracks and make it homelike.

Karl said, " Do whatever you want to, even if it's stupid! Come on, fellows! Let's go on out and capture musk oxen."

But Bill was so full after eating more lunch than anyone else that he didn't feel like capturing musk oxen.

"Then you'll have to stay around the cave and beat the

women and children," Karl said. "The main thing is for you to have something to do."

"Just let him try," said Britta.

But Bill was so full that he lay down in the grass in front of the cave. He stayed there all the time Karl and Olaf were hunting musk oxen and we were sweeping the cave. Then Karl and Olaf came back and let out an awful howl—to show that the hunt had been successful, Karl said. Karl said that it was a Stone-Age howl, and that people howled that way when they were hunting musk oxen in the Stone Age. He bragged about how dangerous it was to hunt them, and said he had got a whole lot. We couldn't see any, though.

Then it started to rain, so we sat in the cave and had such a nice time. The sky was so dark that we thought the weather probably wouldn't get sunny again that day. But then, all of a sudden, the sun came out from behind a cloud. So we left the cave and looked out over the lake. The sun shone on a big stone slab on an island in the middle of the lake, where we go swimming sometimes, and it looked so pretty. Karl said, "Let's row out there and take a swim."

It hadn't been more than two days since we had asked Mommy if we could go swimming soon, and she had said, "No, it's too early. You'll have to wait a little longer."

79

"Well, we *have* waited a little longer," Karl said.

So we rowed over to the island. We undressed on the stone slab and had a race to see who could get into the water first. Bill won. His lunch must have sunk down some.

But the water was so cold that we all came out very quickly. The first thing we saw when we came back to the stone slab was the angry ram from North Farm. He can't be kept in a pasture with the other sheep, because he jumps over all the fences and butts everyone he sees. In the spring he is usually kept out on the island by himself. It's an awful job to get him there. Uncle Erik and Daddy and Uncle Nils help one another to tie his feet with rope; then they put him in the rowboat, and Uncle Erik rows him out to the island and turns him loose. We had forgotten about him and were very surprised when we came out of the water and saw the ram standing on the shore, staring at us. Ulrik is the ram's name.

"Oh, for goodness' sake!" said Anna. "I'd forgotten all about Ulrik."

I think Ulrik thinks it's terribly embarrassing to be tied up like that and put in a boat, with his wives and all the lambs looking on. Perhaps that's why he's usually so angry. Also, it's probably dull to walk around on that little island all alone.

Now he seemed even angrier than usual. He lowered his head and rushed toward us, and Olaf got such a push that he fell down. But he got up again and ran for dear life. So did the rest of us. Bill and Anna and Britta climbed up on a high stone; Olaf and I climbed up in a tree; and Karl hid behind a bush.

I yelled to Karl, "All right, you're so clever at catching musk oxen! Here is one for you—almost. Show us now how you can catch him."

And Anna and Britta cried, "Yes, here comes the musk ox, Karl; catch him now!"

But Karl didn't dare answer, because he was standing behind the bush, and, if he spoke, Ulrik would know he was there.

Ulrik was furious because he couldn't get at us. He stood under the tree where Olaf and I were and butted it until the bark flew. When that didn't do any good, he went over to the high stone where Bill and Britta and

Anna were. He stood below and glared at them as hard as he could.

"Go ahead and glare!" said Britta.

But then we started to wonder how we were going to get away from there. Ulrik didn't look as if he was going to leave.

"Gee, I wish I had something to eat," Bill said.

We had hidden what was left from the lunch in the Rumble-hole, and, now that Bill started talking about it, we were hungry too.

"Have you gone to sleep behind that bush?" Olaf called to Karl. Then Karl stuck his head out and looked around and tried to sneak over to the stone where Bill and Anna and Britta were. But he should never have done that, because, when he did, Ulrik saw him. He rushed toward Karl who started to run very fast. We all yelled, because it looked so terrible to see him running around in the juniper bushes, chased by Ulrik.

"Run, Karl, run!" Anna yelled.

"That's just what I'm doing," Karl yelled.

Once Ulrik pushed Karl and he fell. Then we all yelled so, it sounded like the Stone-Age howl. I think the howl must have scared Ulrik a little. Karl got up and ran on. Ulrik started after him, and we yelled still more, but it didn't help.

There is an old barn on the island with the roof falling in, so it isn't used any more. The door was wide open. Karl ran in there. Ulrik ran in too. Then I started to cry and said, "Oh, Ulrik will gore Karl to death there in the barn."

But then, all of a sudden, we saw Karl come climbing up through the hole in the roof. He jumped down to the ground and ran to close the door of the barn.

"The musk ox is caught," he said.

So, at last, we dared come down. And we all climbed up on the roof and looked down at Ulrik through the hole. Bill said, "You nasty old ram, you!"

And I said, "I hope Pontus never turns into a mean old ram like that!"

Then we had to go home. Karl told us all to get into the rowboat. He said he would open the door of the barn and then, before Ulrik understood what was going on, he would rush down and throw himself into the rowboat. He said that even if Ulrik was an angry old ram, you couldn't leave him locked in the barn where he would starve to death.

We did as Karl said. We always do.

As we rowed away from the island, Ulrik stood on the shore and looked as if he felt very sad that we had left.

"Just tell me if there are any more musk oxen that you

want captured," Karl said, looking smart.

But we didn't want any more musk oxen captured that day. We were so tired and hungry we just wanted to get home.

"I'll see if Mommy has anything to eat," Bill said.

12. The Cherry Company

ANNA may be right after all, that we have the most
fun in the summer. But I like to go to school too,
and when Miss Johnson says good-by to us the last day I
almost cry, because I know that I won't see her for such a
long time. But I soon forget about this, because it's so
wonderful to have summer vacation.

The first evening of our summer vacation we usually
go fishing at the North Farm lake. There's hardly anything that feels as summery as fishing. We make the
rods ourselves of hazel branches, but we get lines and
floats and sinkers and hooks from the store at Big Village.

Karl calls the night we finish school the Big Fishing
Night. There is a rock that's not too big and not too
small where we sit to fish. It's called the Perch Rock,
Anna says, because you never catch any perch there. The
only thing you catch is mosquito bites. But Bill did catch

a big perch the last time we were there. Britta caught two small roaches.

Later, Anna and I sat on our kitchen steps and counted mosquito bites. I had fourteen on my right leg and five on my left. Anna had nine on each leg.

"You could use that for a problem in arithmetic," Anna said. "Let's write it down for Miss Johnson: 'If Lisa has fourteen mosquito bites on one leg and five on the other, and Anna has nine on each leg, who has the most mosquito bites, and how many do they have altogether?' "

But suddenly we remembered that it was summer vacation—and it's silly to do arithmetic then. So we just scratched our bites and had fun until bedtime. How wonderful it is to have summer vacation! One thing we did last summer was to organize a Cherry Company.

We have lots of cherry trees in our garden and in Anna's and Britta's garden. In Olaf's garden there aren't any, at least none that are any good. The South Farm garden has, instead, a tree with fine August pears, and two trees with little delicious yellow plums. The largest cherry tree in the world, I think, is outside Grandfather's window. We call it "Grandfather's cherry tree." Its branches droop down almost to the ground, and every summer it's full of big cherries. Grandfather says that we may eat as many as we want to, but we mustn't pick the cherries from the lowest branches because they are for Kerstin. Grandfather wants Kerstin to be able to pick them herself. And she can too, although she's very little. But Olaf has to watch her, or she'll swallow the pits too. We do as Grandfather says and don't pick any cherries from Kerstin's branches. It is so easy for us to climb up in the tree and pick there. There are many good branches and many forks in the branches where you can sit and eat all you want. Our stomachs hurt a little every year during the cherry season. After the cherries are all gone, we don't have stomach aches any more until the plums get ripe.

Mommy always dries the cherries and keeps them through the winter. She puts them on a cookie sheet in the oven when it's just barely warm. Then the cherries get dry and wrinkled and you can save them to make fruit soup during the winter.

Karl and Bill and I each have a cherry tree of our own. This year they all had an unbelievable amount of cherries.

Although Britta and Anna and Olaf helped us, we couldn't possibly eat all the cherries on our trees. One day Karl was going to dry some, and he filled a whole cookie sheet and put it in the oven. Then he went swimming and forgot all about his cherries. When he looked at them again they had turned into tiny black burned seeds.

"That's not the right way to treat cherries," he said.

Then one night we were up in Grandfather's room, reading the paper and it said that in Stockholm cherries cost two crowns a quart. Karl was very upset to think that he didn't have his cherry tree in Stockholm.

"Then I'd sell my cherries on a street corner and become as rich as the king," he said.

We tried to figure out how much money we would earn if only our cherry trees were in Stockholm. It was so much that Karl turned quite pale when he thought about it.

"If only I had the North Farm lake in the Sahara Desert, I could sell water for two crowns a quart also," said Britta, who thought Karl was silly.

I think Karl lay awake that night and thought and thought about getting two crowns a quart for cherries in Stockholm, because the next day he said he was going to open a cherry store on the highway that runs on the other side of Big Village. There are a great many cars passing there.

"And who knows, some crazy Stockholmers might even come by," he said.

Bill and I said we wanted to sell our cherries too. So

we made a company that we called the Cherry Company. We let Britta and Anna and Olaf be members too, because they helped us to pick our cherries although they did not have any trees of their own.

We got up at five o'clock one morning and started picking. By eight o'clock we had three large baskets of cherries. Then we all ate a lot of oatmeal, so that we'd be able to go without food for a long while and started out toward Big Village. We went by Uncle Emil's store and bought many brown paper bags with some money we had borrowed from Bill's piggy bank.

"What do you think you're going to do now?" Uncle Emil asked.

"We're going to sell cherries," Karl said.

We had left Olaf watching the baskets on the steps outside the store.

"Cherries, now that's something I like," Uncle Emil said. "Perhaps you'll sell some to me?"

Wasn't that good? Uncle Emil measured out two quarts for himself and gave us two crowns for them. He said that a crown a quart was the price for cherries in these parts and that it was a good thing for us to know. Bill got back the money we had borrowed from his piggy bank, and we still had some left. Uncle Emil gave us some candy. When Olaf saw this through the glass in

90

the door, he came rushing into the store as if he had had ants in his pants. When he had got his piece of candy, he rushed out again almost as fast.

We thanked Uncle Emil, and when we got outside, we saw that Olaf was picking up some cherries that he had spilled in the grass.

"What are you *doing*?" Karl said angrily.

"I—I'm just polishing your cherries," Olaf said and sounded scared.

But he had only spilled a few, so it didn't matter.

The highway runs very close to Big Village. In the fall and winter you see practically nothing on it but trucks. In the summer, though, many cars pass by, because people want to see how beautiful the scenery is here.

"How can they see anything at all, when they drive so fast?" said Karl as the first car zoomed past.

We had made a big sign that said CHERRIES, and we held it up every time a car came by. But the cars just drove on. Karl said the people in them probably thought it said DRIVE CAREFULLY, and that was why they rushed by. But Bill thought it was fun to see the cars going so fast. He almost forgot the cherries. His eyes were perfectly round from staring, and he knew the make of every car.

Karl got mad because the cars didn't stop and he said,

"I'll teach them!"

So when the next car started coming he jumped out in the middle of the road and held up the sign. He didn't jump out of the way until the very last minute before he would have been run over. The car stopped with a dreadful squealing of brakes, and a man got out and grabbed Karl by the arm. He said he'd give him a beating that he'd never forget.

"Don't you ever try anything like that again," he said.

92

Karl promised not to do it again, and then, do you know, the man bought a quart of cherries from us before he went on.

There was an awful lot of dust on the road. We had covered the cherries with paper, which was probably a good thing, but we couldn't very well cover ourselves. And every time a car drove by, a whole cloud of dust fell on us.

"What awful dust!" I said.

Karl asked why I had said that. "Why don't you say 'What awful sunshine!' or 'What awful birdsong!'?" he wondered. Anyway, who said we had to like the sunshine and not like dust? So we decided we would like the dust. When the next car went by, and all the dust whirled around us so that we could hardly see each other, Karl said, "What wonderful dust!"

And Britta said, "Yes, there's so much lovely dust on this road—really lovely!"

And Bill said, "I only wish there was a lot more dust."

He didn't have to wait long for his wish to come true. A big truck came thundering by, and I didn't know there was so much dust in the whole world as whirled up behind the truck. Anna stood right in the middle of it and stretched her arms in the air and said, "What wonderful, wonderful dust!"

But then she started to cough, so she couldn't say anything more. When the dust had settled a little we looked at each other; all of us were gray-black.

Although the dust was wonderful, we thought it was a shame that no cars wanted to stop. But finally Karl discovered that we were standing at a stupid place—right in the middle of a straight stretch where the cars were going at high speed. We should move to a curve in the road, he said. So we placed ourselves a little farther away where there were two bends in the road, one right after the other. Then we got the idea of standing in a long row along the side of the road and holding one another by the hand and swinging our arms when a car approached.

"This'll do the trick!" Karl said.

And it did. Almost every car stopped. In the first car that came there were a mother and father and four children, and all the children cried for cherries. Their father bought three quarts, and their mother said, "Wasn't it lucky we found you! We were so hungry and thirsty!"

They bought the little black cherries from my tree. The father told us that they were going far, far away—all the way to a foreign country.

"Isn't it strange," I said, "that my cherries are going abroad while I am staying right here in Noisy Village?"

But Karl said, "Don't be silly! The children will have eaten the cherries long before they get to the foreign country."

But I said, "Even if the cherries were in the tummies of those children, they would go abroad anyway."

Finally we had sold every cherry. We had thirty crowns in the cigar box that we had taken along to keep the money in. It was the Wizards' Chest, which finally had come to some sensible use. Thirty crowns was a terrific lot of money! We divided it so that we got five crowns each.

"And now that you don't have any cherries left, you may eat as many as you like in our garden," Britta said.

"And I'll give you plums, as soon as they're ripe," Olaf said when he got his five crowns.

So you have to admit that the money was fairly divided.

On our way home we went to the confectioner's shop in Big Village and ate a piece of cake each and drank soda pop. We could afford to buy that much. We decided to save the rest of the money.

When we came home and Mommy caught sight of Karl and Bill and me, she threw up her hands and said that she had never seen such a dirty Cherry Company. She wanted us to go out to the laundry room and wash.

But just then Anna came and cried, "What luck! The Finnish bath is heated!"

Britta and Anna had a Finnish bath down by the lake. We took along clean clothes and ran through the cow pasture, as fast as we could.

In the lake we washed off all the wonderful dust. Then we sat in the Finnish bath to sweat. We decided we were going to make a Plum Company too, a little later.

It's awfully hot in the Finnish bath, and finally we were so warm that we almost burst. Then we ran out and cooled off in the lake. My, how wonderful it felt! We splashed water on each other and swam and dived. And when we came up there was no wonderful dust left, not even in our hair.

The weather was so beautiful. We sat on the shore and sunbathed. Karl said, "What awful sunshine!"

And then Olaf laughed and said, "What awful birdsong!"

13. Anna and I Are Going to Be Baby-Nurses—Perhaps

ONE DAY last summer the pastor in Big Village invited everyone in Noisy Village to a large birthday party. Well, he didn't invite the children, but Mommy and Daddy and Uncle Erik were invited—and all the other grownups, even Grandfather. Aunt Lisa felt badly, because she didn't think that she could go because of Kerstin. Then Anna and I said we could look after her. We were going to be baby-nurses when we grew up, so it would be a good thing if we started practicing right away.

"But do you have to practice on my sister?" Olaf said.

He would have liked to look after Kerstin himself, but he had to milk the South Farm cows and feed the pigs and chickens while his mother and father were at the party. Britta would have liked to help too, but she was in bed with a terrible cold.

Aunt Lisa was very happy when we told her what we

wanted to do, but Anna and I were even happier. I pinched Anna's arm and said, "Won't it be fun?"

And Anna pinched me back and said, "I wish they'd hurry and leave soon, so we could start."

But it always takes a terribly long time for people to get ready for a party—except Grandfather. He was ready at six o'clock in the morning, although they weren't supposed to leave until ten. He was all dressed up in his black Sunday suit and his best white shirt. As soon as Uncle Erik had hitched up the horses, Grandfather went to the North Farm wagon and sat down to wait. This was even before Aunt Greta had started to put on her party dress.

Aunt Lisa kept on giving us all sorts of instructions until the very last minute, and then Daddy and Uncle Nils and Uncle Erik smacked their horses, and they all drove off.

Aunt Lisa had said that we should let Kerstin be outdoors as much as possible, because she was the least trouble there. At noon she should have her lunch which was all ready to heat; after that, she should take a nap for a couple of hours.

"Won't that be fun!" Anna said.

"Yes," I said. "I'm sure I'm going to be a baby-nurse when I grow up."

"Me too," said Anna. "It's really easy to take care of children. All you have to do is remember to speak softly and kindly to them. Then they mind you. I read that in the newspaper the other day."

"Yes, of course," I said.

"But you know there are people who yell at their children," Anna said. "And those children never mind their parents, and they grow up to be real little brats. It said that in the paper."

"Who would want to yell at such a sweet little thing?" I said, and tickled Kerstin's foot.

Kerstin sat on a blanket on the lawn and looked happy. She has such a round little forehead, and her eyes are bright blue. In her mouth she has four teeth upstairs and four down, which look just like grains of rice when she laughs. The only thing she can say is "Hi, hi," and she says that almost all the time. Perhaps she means different things every time but you never know.

Sometimes Kerstin rides in a wooden wagon.

"How about taking her for a ride?" Anna suggested. So we did.

"Come here, Kerstin, dear," Anna said and put her down in the wagon. "Now we are going to go for a little ride."

She spoke very softly and kindly, just the way you

should to little children.

"There now, aren't you nice and comfy?" she said.

But Kerstin didn't think so at all. She started to stand straight up in the wagon and jump up and down and say "Hi, hi," but, of course, we couldn't let her do that.

"I think we'd better tie her down," I said. So we did—with a heavy piece of cord. But then Kerstin started to howl so loud you could hear it a mile away.

Olaf came running from the barn and said, "What are you doing to my little sister?"

"Nothing, stupid," I said. "We are just speaking softly and kindly to her!"

"Well, that's all right," Olaf said. "But also you'd better let her do what she likes, so she won't cry."

We thought Olaf should know how his sister should be taken care of, so we let Kerstin stand up in the wagon and say "Hi, hi," all she wanted. I would pull the wagon while Anna ran along beside Kerstin to catch her every time she fell. Then we came to a deep ditch, and when Kerstin saw it, she climbed out of the wagon.

"Let's see what she is going to do," Anna said.

Well, she showed us all right! There's something odd about little children. You think that their legs are too short to run very fast, but that's where you're wrong. A little child can run as fast as a rabbit if he tries to. At least, Kerstin can. She said "Hi, hi," and ran right into the ditch before we had time to wink an eye. There she stumbled and fell on her head in the water. It's true that Olaf had said we should let her do what she wanted to, and she wanted to lie in the ditch, but we still thought we'd better pull her out. She was sopping wet and yelling at the top of her voice. She scowled at us as if it had been our fault that she had fallen in. But we spoke softly and kindly to her and put her back in the wagon. We pulled her home to get some dry clothes, and she yelled the whole time. Olaf got furious when he saw how Kerstin looked.

"What do you think you're doing anyway?" he shouted. "Did you try to drown her?"

Then Anna said that he should speak softly and kindly to us, because we were children too—except we were big ones, of course.

But Kerstin went over and threw her arms around Olaf's legs and cried and cried, so Anna and I felt just as if we *had* tried to drown her.

Olaf helped us find some clean clothes for Kerstin. But then he had to go down to the barn again.

We put Kerstin's best dress on, because Olaf hadn't been able to find any other. It was so pretty—white with tiny little tucks and ruffles.

"You have to be very careful of this dress," I said to Kerstin, but it was quite evident that she didn't understand what I said, because she ran right over to the stove and got a big soot-spot right in the middle of her dress. "Hi, hi," she said. We brushed it off as well as we could, but it was impossible to get much of it off. Kerstin laughed when we brushed her. She probably thought that we were playing a game.

"It's twelve o'clock," Anna said all of a sudden. "It's time for Kerstin to have her lunch."

We hurried to heat up her spinach in a saucepan on the stove. I took Kerstin on my lap, and Anna fed her.

She ate very well and opened her mouth so nicely that Anna said, "She really is an awfully nice little kid."

Then Kerstin said "Hi, hi," and hit the spoon down on the table. All of the spinach flew into my eyes.

Anna laughed until she almost dropped the plate, and I got mad at her. Kerstin laughed, too, but she probably didn't know why Anna was laughing. She must think that it's quite natural for people to have spinach between the eyes.

Then all of a sudden, when she didn't want to eat any more, she closed her mouth tight and hit the spoon on the table again and again so that more than half of her spinach got on her dress. We gave her some fruit soup to drink from a cup, and more than half of that got on her dress too.

After that, the beautiful dress wasn't white any longer but green and red with just a little bit of white in certain spots.

"There's one thing I'm happy about," Anna said, "and that is that it's time for Kirsten to take a nap now."

"Yes, that's one thing I'm happy about too," I said.

And then we took off all of Kerstin's clothes again and put on her pajamas. When we had finally finished, we were worn out.

"We're the ones who need to take a nap, not Kerstin,"

I said to Anna.

But we put Kerstin in her crib and went out of the nursery and closed the door. Then Kerstin started howling as loudly as she could. We tried to pretend that we didn't hear her, but she cried louder and louder until finally Anna stuck her head through the door and said, "Be quiet, you little brat!"

Of course we knew that you should speak softly and kindly to little children, but sometimes you just can't. But what the paper said was probably right: that children become regular little brats when you yell at them. At least Kerstin did. She cried louder than ever. Then we both went into her room. She was happy as soon as she saw us and stood up in her crib; she jumped up and down and said "Hi, hi," the whole time we were in there. And she stuck her little hand out between the bars and patted me. When I leaned over the crib, she laid her cheek against mine.

"She's awfully cute, in spite of everything," I said.

Then Kerstin bit my cheek, so I had a mark for two days.

We laid her down in the crib and tried to tuck the blanket around her, but she kicked it off. When she had kicked it off ten times, we didn't pay any more attention to her. We just said, "Sleep well now, dear," very softly and kindly. Then we went out and closed the door. Right away she started howling again.

"Enough is enough," Anna said. "Let her yell!"

We sat down at the kitchen table and tried to talk, but we couldn't because Kerstin yelled louder and louder and louder. Sometimes she was quiet for a couple of seconds but that was only when she took a breath for the next howl.

"Perhaps she has an ache somewhere," I said.

"Goodness, what if she has a stomach ache," Anna said. "It could be appendicitis, or something."

So we *ran* into Kerstin's room. She stood up in bed, and her eyes were filled with tears, but as soon as she saw us, she said "Hi, hi," and started to jump up and down and laugh.

"That kid doesn't have a stomach ache or any other kind of ache," Anna said. "Come on, let's go!"

So we closed the door and sat down by the kitchen table again, listening to Kerstin howl louder and louder. Finally she got quiet.

"Oh, how wonderful," I said. "She has finally gone to sleep."

Anna and I took out Olaf's Old Maid game and sat down and played Old Maid, and it was very nice.

"Babies should stay in bed all the time. Then, at least,

you know where they are," Anna said.

Then we heard a strange noise from the nursery. It sounded like a little happy mumble, the kind of sound that children make when they are doing something pleasant.

"No, now this is going too far," I said. "It can't be possible that she's *still* awake!"

We tiptoed up and peeked carefully through the keyhole. We could see Kerstin's crib, but we couldn't see Kerstin. Her crib was empty. We rushed into the nursery. And guess where Kerstin was! She was sitting in the open fireplace that had been beautiful, before Kerstin got there. It wasn't exactly beautiful any longer, because Kerstin was sitting in the middle of it with a jar of shoe polish in her hand. She was black with shoe polish from head to toe. She had shoe polish in her hair and shoe polish all over her face and shoe polish on her hands and on her pajamas and on her feet, and all of the fireplace was decorated with shoe polish. Probably Uncle Nils had stood by the fireplace to polish his shoes before the party and then hadn't put the cover back on the jar.

"Hi, hi," Kerstin said when she saw us.

"Did it say in the paper whether you could spank little children?" I said.

"I don't remember," said Anna.

107

Then Kerstin stood up and ran toward Anna, and Anna yelled even louder than she did, *"Don't touch me, you brat!"*

Kerstin did anyway. Anna grabbed her hands but still got shoe polish all over herself. Then I laughed just as hard at Anna as she had at me when I had got the spinach between my eyes.

"Aunt Lisa won't know her child when she sees her," I said, when I had stopped laughing.

We didn't know how to wash off shoe polish, so we decided to ask Britta. Anna, who was already smeared, would stay and hold Kerstin while I went to ask her.

When I told Britta what Kerstin had done, she said, "Well, you're just fine baby-nurses!" Then she blew her nose and turned toward the wall and said that she was sick and didn't know how you washed off shoe polish.

In the meantime Olaf had come from the barn, and he went absolutely wild when he saw Kerstin.

"Are you out of your minds," he yelled. "Have you painted her black?"

We tried to explain to him that it wasn't our fault. But Olaf was furious and said that there should be a law against people like us becoming baby-nurses, and, in any case, we'd have to get another child to practice on.

But we all helped one another to fill a tub with warm water. Then we carried it out on the lawn and led Kerstin out to it. When she walked across the floor, she left cute little black footprints. We put her in the tub and scrubbed her thoroughly from top to toe. We washed her hair too. She got a little soap in her eyes, and then she yelled so loudly you could hear it all over Noisy Village. Karl and Bill came running and asked if we were slaughtering pigs.

"No," Olaf said. "It's just these two fine baby-nurses who are practicing."

We couldn't get the shoe polish really off, and when we had finished scrubbing and drying Kerstin, she was a

peculiar gray color all over. But she was happy anyway. She ran around on the lawn, stark naked, and yelled "Hi, hi," and laughed so you could see every tooth in her mouth. Olaf said, "Isn't she a darling baby?"

We thought that the gray color would probably wear off in time so the pink child who was underneath would show up again. It would be around Christmas time, Karl thought.

Afterward Olaf put Kerstin to bed. She didn't say boo, just stuck her thumb in her mouth and went to sleep.

110

"That's the way to take care of children," Olaf said. Then he went to feed the pigs.

Anna and I sat down on the kitchen steps to rest.

"Poor Aunt Lisa, who has it like this every day," I said.

"Do you know what I think?" Anna said. "I think all that in the paper was a lie, because it doesn't make any difference *how* you talk to little children. Whether you talk softly and kindly or yell at them, they still do exactly as they please."

After that we were quiet a while.

"Anna, are you going to be a baby-nurse when you grow up?" I said finally.

"Perhaps," Anna said. But then she looked thoughtful and stared out over the barn roof and said, "Well, I really don't know."

14. Midsummer in Noisy Village

AND now the last thing I want to tell you about is
what we did on Midsummer Eve, the twenty-third
of June. In the South Farm meadow we had a Midsummer pole. Everybody in the whole village helped to make

it. First we rode way out into the forest in our wagon to pick leaves that we were going to use. Daddy drove, and even Kerstin was allowed to come along. She was so happy that she laughed and laughed. Olaf gave her a little branch to hold in her hand, and she sat and waved it back and forth. And Olaf sang this old song for her:

"Kerstin had a little gold coach
In which she was going to ride;
A little gold whip she held in the air
And greeted each passer with smiles so fair..."

All the rest of us sang too. Agda had come along to help us pick leaves and she sang:

"Now it is summer;
Now there is sunshine;
Now there are flowers and leaves..."

When we came home from the forest, Agda, Britta, Anna, and I picked a big bunch of lilacs from the bushes behind our woodshed. Then we took them over to the South Farm meadow, where Oscar and Kalle had already cut the pole. We tied the leaves all around the pole and hung two big wreaths of lilacs from the crossbar at the top. Then we raised the pole and danced around it. Uncle Erik, Anna's daddy, plays the accordion well, and he played a lot of gay tunes for us all to dance to—all except Grandfather and Kerstin. Grandfather sat in a chair and

Kerstin sat in his lap at first. But she couldn't keep from pulling his beard, so her daddy put her up on his shoulders. In that way, Kerstin could dance with us too. Poor Grandfather couldn't dance, but I don't think he was sorry. He just said, "My, oh my, it seems longer ago than yesterday that I danced around a Midsummer pole.

Then we all sat down in the grass and drank coffee that Mommy and Aunt Greta and Aunt Lisa had made. We had buns and cookies too. Grandfather drank three cups of coffee, because that's something he really likes.

"Coffee is something I have to have," he says.

I don't like it at all, but when you drink it while sitting in the grass in Midsummer, it tastes much better than usual.

We played The Last Pair Out and a lot of other games. It's such fun when the mommies and daddies play with us. It would probably not be so much fun if we had to play with them every day, but when it's Midsummer, I think they should be allowed to play too. Skipp ran around and barked while we played. I think he thought it was fun too.

We were allowed to stay up just as long as we wanted to that evening. Agda said if you climbed over nine fences before you went to bed, and if you picked nine kinds of flowers and put them under your pillow, you'd dream at night about the one you would marry.

Britta and Anna and I thought it would be lots of fun to climb over nine fences, although we already know who we are going to marry. I'm going to marry Olaf, and Britta and Anna are going to marry Karl and Bill.

"Are you going to climb over nine fences?" Karl said to

Britta. "Well, go ahead, by all means. But please dream about someone else but me. Not that I'm superstitious, but it *might* help."

"Yes, let's hope you don't dream about us," Bill said.

"Yes, let's *certainly* hope so," Olaf said.

The boys are stupid and don't want to marry us.

Agda said that you had to be very quiet while you climbed over the fences. You couldn't laugh or talk at all the whole time.

"If you can't talk the whole time, Lisa," Karl said, "then you might as well go to bed."

"Why?" I said.

"Because you can't climb nine fences in two minutes, and you've never been quiet longer than that in your life—except the time you had the mumps, of course."

We didn't pay any attention to the boys but just started climbing. We began with the fence around the South Farm meadow and came into the birch woods behind it. It's strange in the woods when it's dark. Well, it wasn't perfectly dark, just rather twilightish and still. It was very quiet, because the birds had stopped chirping, and it smelled so good from all the trees and flowers. We each picked a flower when we had climbed over the first fence.

There is one thing that I don't understand and that's

why you always get the giggles when you know that you're not supposed to laugh. As soon as we had climbed over the first fence, we started. The boys came climbing after us just to tease us and make us laugh.

"Don't step in the mud puddle," Bill said to Anna.

"There's no puddle—" Anna said. But then she remembered that she wasn't supposed to talk. Then Britta and Anna and I giggled, and the boys laughed out loud.

"You can't giggle like that," Karl said. "Remember that you're not supposed to laugh."

Then we giggled still more. And the boys ran around us and pulled our hair and pinched our arms to make us laugh. We couldn't say anything because we weren't supposed to talk.

"Ubbelibubbelimuck," Karl said.

It wasn't a bit funny, really, but Britta and Anna and I couldn't keep from laughing. I stuffed my handkerchief in my mouth, but that didn't help; my laughter came chirping out anyway. But when we had climbed over the ninth fence, and picked our ninth flowers, we stopped laughing and were just mad at the boys for spoiling everything for us.

I put the flowers under my pillow anyway. I had a buttercup and a bird's foot and a bluebell and a daisy and an almond flower and a rockrose and a violet and two other flowers that I don't know the names of. I didn't dream anything at all that night, and I'm certain that it was because those silly boys had made us laugh.

But I'm going to marry Olaf anyway, so there!

About the Author

Though best known for her books about the mischievous and larger-than-life Pippi Longstocking, author Astrid Lindgren, born in 1907, wrote numerous other books about children and family life that were more conventional. Her writing was greatly influenced by a vividly remembered childhood on a farm called Naas in southern Sweden. Here she met a surprising variety of people whose characters later enriched both her "real" stories and her fairy tales, a number of which, as in the stories of Noisy Village, also reflect the rural serenity of Smaaland as it was when she was a child.

Astrid Lindgren showed a talent for writing early in her life but she purposely decided that she would never write a book. Nevertheless, after her marriage to Sture Lindgren in 1931, she did begin telling stories from her childhood to her two children, Lars and Karin. It was Karin, sick with pneumonia, who one day said to her mother, "Tell me about Pippi Longstocking," and thus was born the character who became the focus of many family storytelling sessions and, later, the star of Astrid Lindgren's first book. For after falling and spraining her ankle one winter, Mrs. Lindgren finally changed her mind about writing and set down the tales of Pippi for her daughter's tenth birthday in 1944. This manuscript went on to win first prize in a contest and the prolific career of writing was launched.

Astrid Lindgren was honored many times in many ways during the course of her lifetime, winning the prestigious Hans Christian Andersen Medal in 1958, and receiving the tribute of a set of commemorative Swedish stamps designed by illustrators of her books upon her eightieth birthday.

In her acceptance speech (published in *Bookbird)* for the Hans Christian Andersen Medal she said, "Children work miracles when they read. They take our poor sentences and words and give them a life which in themselves they do not have. The author alone does not create all the mystical essence contained within the pages of a book. The reader must help. . . . All great things that have happened in the world, happened first of all in someone's imagination, and the aspect of the world of tomorrow depends largely on the extent of the power of imagination in those who are just now learning to read. This is why children must have books, and why there must be people ... who really care what kind of books are put into the children's hands."

There are many imaginative ways of feeding a child's imagination. We have much to be grateful for in Astrid Lindgren's appealing portrayal of a simple rural life of another day in her Noisy Village books, as well as in her humorous and fanciful tales that so effortlessly carry children into worlds beyond their own.

Astrid Lindgren died on January 28th, 2002 at the age of 94.

About the Illustrator

Ilon Wikland's charming pictures, line drawings and watercolors illustrate many of Astrid Lindgren's works. Miss Wikland, a refugee from Estonia, came to Sweden in 1944. She started drawing as a hobby during a long stay in the hospital, before going on to study in a school of advertising and book design. In 1954 she met Astrid Lindgren, who was looking for an artist to illustrate *Mio, My Son*. Thus began a long series of collaborated books.

Miss Wikland, who has reached so many children by her pictorial art, said of the author, "Astrid writes so that I, for one, see before me a constant flow of images. Working with that kind of text is of enormous help to an illustrator." In turn, Astrid Lindgren wrote to her illustrator, reflecting on their decades-long association, "I do know one thing for certain, and that is how indebted I am to you; how important you have been to my stories in helping them to reach their audience through your pictures. Many children will remember your creations all their lives. I thank you from the bottom of my heart." So inseparable have pictures and text become, as in the case of the Noisy Village series, it is difficult to think of one without the other. We are all indebted to this author and illustrator for their rich, cooperative depiction of the precocity and joy of childhood, a true gift to the world of children's literature.